Dealing with

S omeone has said that grief is
by shortcuts. No two people
deal with grief one way or anoth
relationship, the greater the loss.

I will never forget one of the first funerals I took as a young
minister. The casket was carried in by only one man. It had inside
it a baby girl who had died. A few minutes into the short service, the
mother ran forward, threw herself on the coffin and screamed at
the top of her voice. Who can measure how wrung-out and exhausted
she was by those days of grief?

If you are reading this in the first few
days or weeks after the death of a loved
one, you may be in shock, and you will
need—when the busy funeral process is
over—to rest well and talk well. You need

Grief is a process that cannot be reduced by shortcuts

to recognize that your whole system has been through trauma. It's
an exhausting experience. To deal well with the tragedy—and I don't
mean quickly—you will need to be looked after. You will need to
be able to share your emotions in words with a good listener.

Whatever the emotions that do surface, we do well to acknowledge
them and seek to channel them constructively. Perhaps you are filled
with anger for something that has happened. There is proper anger
that expresses itself in talking, praying and crying, but there is also
destructive anger that expresses itself in revenge and payback. The
person who can speak of their feelings to someone who will listen
and gently steer the process is more likely to deal well with things.

If you are feeling guilty about the events surrounding a recent
tragedy, try to sort out true guilt from false guilt. Much false guilt
surrounds a death. Who can escape thoughts that we could have
done more, cared more or even prevented more? If you did what
you could, this is not the time to add false guilt to loss. Emotions
tend to get mixed up at a time like this.

However, we must also face the possibility of real guilt. It may
be that you have done something that you are not proud of, that
was wrong, either in connection with the person you have lost, or

more generally. And your right and understandable response to this realization is the pang of guilt.

If there is real guilt (simple or serious), then a way must be found to deal with it. This is a problem that humans have always struggled with. How can a guilty conscience be put at ease? The Bible provides the most comprehensive and powerful answer ever given to that question. It says that real guilt—the deep and painful kind that comes from having done something that you really know is wrong—comes not only from having let another person down; at a deeper level it comes from having let our Creator down, from having sinned against God. And accordingly, we can only have our consciences cleansed from guilt by being forgiven by God.

The experience of loss and grief can be a catalyst for helping us face these big issues of sin and guilt and forgiveness in our lives. The Christian writer C. S. Lewis once said that Jesus Christ often comes to our attention in our youth or carefree days, and 'knocks' at the door of our house. We ignore the opportunity, and treat him as an unwelcome stranger. But because he loves us, he may well come back to our house and get our attention by taking out the back wall or the central staircase. It's not because he's against us but because he's *for* relationship! If he didn't care, he would leave us alone. But because he loves us, he doesn't.

This crisis of conscience may be a serious—even severe—opportunity for you. I'm not suggesting that death or loss is in any way a punishment from God. But it may be a time when refusal to God becomes receptiveness towards God. Many, many people have found that personal tragedy has been the beginning of something new in their lives—the recognition that life is hopeless and helpless without Christ.

I'll say more about this below, but at this point I simply want to say that the process of grief has a healing aspect to it, and this healing may also be spiritual and eternal. As we go through our own "valley of the shadow of death", it may be the time when we finally realize that the person who went through the deepest valley in the universe—to the depths of punishment for sin (ours not his)—is the same person who emerged and who now, as risen King, comes seeking people like us. It seems incredible but it is true. Jesus Christ not only went through death to save us from the things we deserve; he is able to take us through that valley fearing no evil.

At a time like this

Some answers for loss and grief

Simon Manchester

You may not feel very much like reading right now. No words can take away pain, bring people back or make everything right. But sometimes information can change our perspective and provide what we need to know. There are three things in particular that we need to know at a time like this:

- We need to know something of the way that loss and grief affect us. We need to know that we are not alone in the process of **dealing with grief**, and that there is a way through the valley. The feelings we go through—such as numbness, anxiety, anger, guilt, fear and then peace—are normal and good stepping stones.

- We need to know whether there is anyone who can help us understand what has happened; whether there is an **expert** on life and death who might make more sense than all the other voices around us.

- We need some reliable answers to our **questions**. When we are grieving, troubling questions may surface, not only about what has happened, but about the future, about the next world (if there is one), and about God. There are eight significant questions, with corresponding answers, in the third section of this booklet.

My hope is that the words that follow will at least go some way towards informing and comforting you, and showing you a way forward out of the darkness and sorrow you are now experiencing.

The Expert

At funerals I've noticed that there is a common idea that no-one can know about life after death. If someone were to say that they 'know' about the future, they would be seen as arrogant or crazy. At the same time, I've noticed people at funerals describing how the deceased is now in heaven or at peace. Everyone seems to agree that this is right and appropriate. So there is this tension between not knowing anything for sure and saying things as if they are sure.

If this world is like a great 'waiting room' with a door called 'death' nearby, in the tragedies of life, we see young and old, men and women, individuals and groups, going through this door all the time, but not returning to us. We desperately need someone to come back to tell us what is on the other side. All of us are guessers in the waiting room; this is why we are so fascinated by (or suspicious about) people who claim to know how to contact the other side.

> In God's kindness and fairness, he has not left us to be guessers.

When I say to people, "We need an expert—someone who has gone through the grave and come back to tell us what it's all about", some suddenly realize that there is a person who *has* done this. That person is Jesus Christ.

In God's kindness and fairness, he has not left us to be guessers. It is an historical fact that not only did Jesus Christ live in this world and die on a cross, he also went into the grave and came back to prove his authority over the grave. He is an expert on life and death—an expert who has gone across and come back. The evidence for Jesus being this expert is both compelling and encouraging. Let me mention a little of this evidence so that you might move from the position of 'guesser' to 'knower'. This shift will shed bright light on the hard road you are travelling at the moment because, if there is an Expert who can tell us the truth about life and death and God and the future, then this puts everything into a new perspective.

So how do we know that Jesus is this Expert?

Firstly, he **spoke often** of death and life, and foretold his own death and resurrection. The reporters of his day (Matthew, Mark, Luke and John) recorded his repeated promises to go through the grave himself, and to bring life beyond the grave to those who followed him. Here is one example: "I tell you the truth, whoever hears my word and believes him who sent me has eternal life and will not be condemned; he has crossed over from death to life" (John chapter 5, verse 24). If Jesus had failed in these promises, and simply fallen over and died, he would have been exposed as just a talker. But instead thousands—and then millions—devoted themselves to him because he backed up his talk with resurrection from the grave.

> The coming of Jesus was the historical moment that changed the world forever

Secondly, the **empty tomb** of Jesus is good evidence because it cannot be explained satisfactorily unless he rose, as he said he would. There are well-worn alternative explanations for the empty tomb, but none of them stand up to scrutiny. For example, if disciples stole the body, why go preaching that Jesus had risen, and get punished for it? If the Romans stole the body, why not produce it and stop Christianity in its tracks?

Thirdly, his **appearances** balance perfectly the disappearance of his body from the tomb. At his tomb, he persuaded a woman who had come to pay her respects that he was alive by appearing before her in the flesh. Then he began to visit groups of disciples, showing them that what he had promised had come to pass. Some had to be persuaded that this was a real resurrection. The famous 'doubting' disciple, Thomas, needed real proofs (such as real wounds) before he was convinced. Jesus' appearances took place over a specific period of six weeks so that, by the time Jesus had done his work of persuasion, his disciples were ready to live and die for the truth. The church then began to take off. Now millions who hear the facts of Christ and check the evidence for Christ find themselves standing on solid ground and having their lives changed.

Let me be quite clear then about the evidence: it is not only

solid, it is serious. I heard a man on television say recently that he didn't believe in God because, if there was a God, he would have interrupted the process of history. Here was an intelligent man somehow forgetting that the whole process of history *has* been decisively interrupted by Jesus Christ, the man who divides the history of the world into BC and AD.

The coming of Jesus Christ was the historical moment that changed the world forever, and we still publicly celebrate his birth (Christmas), his death (Good Friday) and his resurrection (Easter Day). The events behind the public holidays are very significant and serious. Jesus says that he has complete control over death, and has pioneered the way to life beyond the grave. He has opened the road from here to heaven. We may have huge questions about why people we love die as they do (I attempt some answers below), but one answer can be found which is anchored in our history: death is not the end. Jesus alone can say, "Do not be afraid ... I am the Living One; I was dead, and behold I am alive for ever and ever! And I hold the keys of death ..." (Revelation chapter 1, verses 17-18).

Read the pages of the New Testament and you will see the brilliant way Jesus proved this in his ministry as well as in his own resurrection. The famous Lazarus (in John's Gospel, chapter 11) was permitted by Jesus to die for the specific purpose of showing that Jesus' power goes beyond the sickbed to the grave. He allowed Lazarus to decline and die so that people in every century would know that Jesus is master of the grave. By the time Lazarus was brought out of his tomb, even Jesus' enemies knew that his claim to be "the resurrection and the life" was not a piece of empty talk (John chapter 11, verse 25).

Jesus was so revolutionary that, as he faced a corpse on its deathbed, he could speak of the person as "not dead but asleep" (Mark chapter 5, verse 39). He didn't mean for a minute that the person was not genuinely dead, but that it was a simple thing for him to 'wake' a person and cause them to rise up just as if they had been asleep. It was not Jesus' practice to go about raising all the dead he encountered, but he raised three people in the New Testament to make his power widely and forever known.

I mention all this information not to drag you through old history, but so that you might know that there is a solid foundation beneath the Christian faith which creates hope and peace the more it is considered and examined. The Christian church, or some of its representatives, may be unimpressive, but the foundations for Christianity are very impressive indeed.

What we are asked to do is not to understand every detail of God's ways, but to trust the one who opened the grave for all to go through.

Questions needing answers

So far we have talked in a general way about dealing with grief, and looked at how the answers to our deepest questions and needs can be found by turning to the One who knows all about death and life: Jesus Christ.

But what of our specific questions? Here is a selection of very common questions, along with a brief answer from Jesus Christ, the Expert.

(a) Why has this happened?

Once, when Jesus and his disciples saw a man born blind by the side of the road, the disciples asked Jesus: "Rabbi, who sinned, this man or his parents, that he was born blind?" This was the common view of the time, and it is very often our instinctive reaction to tragedy or suffering. Why? Why has this happened now and to me? What have I done to deserve this? Is God punishing me?

The answer Jesus gives is the answer that the Bible almost always gives to this question: "Neither this man nor his parents sinned" (John chapter 9, verses 1-2). The Bible's **specific** answer to why someone suffers and dies is almost always withheld from us. Even Job, the most famous sufferer in the Bible, cried for answers. And though he was satisfied to trust in a very great God, he was never told the reasons for his losses.

The Bible's **general** answer to why people suffer and die is that we live in a fallen world. This world is not heaven and it is not hell. It is in "bondage to decay" (Romans chapter 8, verse 21). It is dislocated. The human race has turned its back on God's right to decide how we live and so "sin entered the world ... and death through sin" (Romans chapter 5, verse 12). This may seem like a cold and irrelevant answer to someone grieving, but it is the clearest explanation of why our world is as it is. The massive price of turning our backs on God is a breakdown in relationships—with him, with other people and with the 'garden' he has put us in.

One verse of the Bible that has genuinely helped me to face many griefs and to help others face them is Deuteronomy chapter 29, verse 29: "The secret things belong to the LORD our God, but the

things revealed belong to us and to our children for ever". What this means is that while we can remain in the dark about many things (especially the apparent randomness of events and the injustice of so much suffering) we can also be very certain about other things. We can be certain that the God who has made so much beauty, provided so much plenty, and saved so many people out of sheer kindness, has anchored his love in history through Jesus, and given his word that he will bring all things together in justice and glory.

So we don't often know specifically why these things happen. But we *can* know and trust in the God who knows all.

(b) Why would God allow this?

Not long before his death, Jesus warned his disciples that he was about to leave them, if only for a while. In answer to their understandable concern and alarm, Jesus said to them: "Do not let your hearts be troubled. Trust in God; trust also in me" (John chapter 14, verse 1).

The disciples knew Jesus well. They knew what sort of leader he was, and they knew that he had come from God. They had good reason to trust in both God and Jesus, even though they didn't really know what was going to happen or why.

When our knowledge of God's character is shaky, it is easy to lose all confidence in him. Imagine a complete stranger taking a child to a hospital for surgery. To the child, it can seem like a cruel and frightening thing to do. But when a loved and trusted parent takes a child in for surgery, the child has little reason to doubt that someone very loving is doing something that has to be done.

So it is with God. Once we realize that he is by nature "love" (1 John chapter 4, verse 8), we can begin to work on the problems we face. Once, in the midst of a tragic family loss, someone wrote to me the words of Psalm 18, verse 30: "As for God, his way is perfect". It didn't explain everything, but it reminded me of the rock of his character on which I could stand. It reminded me that God might allow something to happen (without explaining the reasons) and still be perfect in love and power.

(c) Where are our loved ones now?

Jesus once said: "My sheep listen to my voice; I know them, and they follow me. I give them eternal life, and they will never perish; no-one can snatch them out of my hand" (John chapter 10, verses 27-28). Someone who trusts in Christ, who is one of Christ's own, will never be snatched out of his hands, even in death. We read elsewhere in the Bible that absolutely nothing—including death—"will be able to separate us from the love of God that is in Christ Jesus" (Romans chapter 8, verses 38-39). As Jesus said to the man being crucified beside him, who had put his trust in Jesus: "today you will be with me in paradise" (Luke chapter 23, verse 43).

With regards to the person whose faith in Christ you are unsure of, or whom you fear was resistant to Christ, don't burden yourself with what you cannot be sure of. We know that Jesus came to "seek and to save what was lost" (Luke chapter 19, verse 10) and that he promised: "whoever comes to me I will never drive away" (John chapter 6, verse 37). God will do what is right, and we can confidently leave it in his hands.

(d) Will I see my loved ones again?

Jesus, the Expert, does not leave us with wishful thinking on this point: "For my Father's will is that everyone who looks to the Son and believes in him shall have eternal life, and I will raise him up at the last day" (John chapter 6, verse 40). On another occasion, Jesus prayed that all those who believe might be "with me where I am, [able] to see my glory" (John chapter 17, verse 24). It was not enough for him just to rise; he will see all his people rise to join him. The Apostle Paul covers all the issues when he writes: "... the one who raised the Lord Jesus from the dead will also raise us with Jesus and present us with you in his presence" (2 Corinthians chapter 4, verse 14).

Just as we have been given a body for this world, so God gives his people a body for the next world—a resurrection body. The only clue we have as to what this might look like is the risen body of Jesus—new and unlimited in its powers but still recognizable and touchable (Luke chapter 24, verse 39). So we expect to see and recognize loved ones who put their trust in Christ, because of God's promises and Jesus' proofs.

(e) What is the next world like?

Imagine trying to describe our world to a baby in the womb. Because of our limitations, Jesus used very simple pictures to describe what the next world would be like. He likens it to a great house (John chapter 14, verse 2) and to a banquet (Matthew chapter 8, verse 11)—to assure us of security and joy.

All that was lost in the Fall of humanity (fellowship with God, with others and a secure place to live) will be replaced in the Resurrection. All that was lost in sin will be made up (and more) in salvation. The description of the new creation in Revelation chapters 21-22 is of a close, joyful fellowship with God and his people, a perfect and permanent home (no boredom!) with every grief removed, and every joy established for eternity.

What we glimpse briefly in this world will be grasped in the next.

(f) Is it right to grieve?

Not only is it right, it is important. It is important to see that Jesus wept (John chapter 11, verse 35), grieving over Lazarus' death even though he was about to raise him back to life! Human death always brings sadness. The loss of a loved one needs to be faced, not avoided, and grief (seen in the perfect person of Christ) is a healthy way to respond. But, in the midst of the grief, there is this concrete 'hope' through Christ that death is not the end.

(g) What should I tell children about death?

Most children have their own simple coping mechanisms, and the implications of death are not so real to them. But we should be careful of passing on fanciful ideas like "he is now an angel", or dangerous ideas like "God took him" or "he's gone away forever". These can come back to haunt people.

Jesus used one image that might be a useful one to share with children. Speaking about his own impending death, he once said: "I tell you the truth, unless a grain of wheat falls to the ground and dies, it remains only a single seed. But if it dies, it produces many seeds" (John chapter 12, verse 24). It's an image that's taken up elsewhere in the Bible as well—the body that is buried in the ground will one day be changed into a new and wonderful form in the Resurrection (1 Corinthians chapter 15, verse 37).

Children need to know that God is good; that he does not punish us in mean or vindictive ways; that everything is under his good control; that the person who died has finished the time that God had for them on earth; and that God will always be faithful and do what is right.

(h) How will I cope from now on?

One hour at a time, one day at a time. God will continue to provide. Jesus spoke of each day having enough trouble of its own, but he also said that his followers are well watched over because "your heavenly Father knows what you need" (Matthew chapter 6, verses 32-34).

Every day, God's "compassions never fail. They are new every morning" (Lamentations chapter 3, verses 22-23). And although there will be waves of grief, and times of painful loss, he will carry you in his everlasting arms (Deuteronomy chapter 33, verse 27).

This is a time to speak frankly—but humbly—to God and ask him to help you trust him, and not turn away from him. The temptation to drown pain in wrongful ways is real. We need to ask him for the strength to deal with pain in wise ways.

The welcome that matters

I once took a funeral and, apart from me, there was just an undertaker. We stood in the rain in a cemetery. By contrast, some funerals are watched by tens or hundreds of thousands. But what is said and done on this side of the river of death is not as important as what is said and done on the other side.

Jesus said that people will arrive and stand before him, and some will hear those unbeatable words, "Come ... take your inheritance" (Matthew chapter 25, verse 34). On the other hand, some will hear those unbearable words, "Depart from me" (Matthew chapter 25, verse 41). The person who had no-one present at their funeral can be welcomed by Jesus (and millions of others), and hear words that no preacher could ever improve on. The person who had television coverage for their funeral can be refused by the one person who really matters.

We are not left to wait and wonder what will happen. God is not so confusing or sadistic as to leave us to battle on and wonder where we will go after this life. He has given us historical proof of a saviour and wonderful promises to stand on.

In the midst of great hurt, it may be difficult to see any point in relating to God, except to gain his comfort. But, along with what has happened to us, we need to face up to what we have done. There is real hurt in our life but there is also real sin. We may have received much pain but we have also caused much pain to God by turning our back on Jesus Christ and his perfect right to say what we should and shouldn't do. We will need to admit that and change. It's a bit like going to a neighbour you've treated very badly and asking for help with a disaster in the kitchen. There needs to be some "sorry" if there is to be some "please". So it is with God.

We also need to recognize that forgiveness is possible, and is only offered, because Jesus Christ died to pay for it. The cross of Christ was a 'swap', where he shouldered our sins and paid the price of punishment for us so that we might receive the acceptance and welcome that he deserved—held out to us by God.

To receive God's forgiveness through Christ, you will need to do more than simply claim it, as if it were like a product. The forgiveness of Christ comes with the person of Christ. You will not be asking just for a piece of paper with 'pardon' written on it, you will be asking for a person who will cleanse you and welcome you. The famous 'prodigal son' (Luke chapter 15, verses 11-32) was a young man, aware of his guilt, who didn't just write home. Instead, he came home to offer himself to the father he had offended and he received a loving welcome.

The Bible also tells us that when Jesus Christ went through death, and rose victorious on the other side, God placed him on the throne of the universe. We need to admit this and surrender to him (Philippians chapter 2, verses 9-11). We need to hand over the keys (so to speak) and agree to cooperate completely.

This 'surrendering' and 'receiving' is what the Bible calls repenting and believing. In doing this, you will be ready to welcome Jesus Christ as your own Lord and Saviour. The Bible says that "to all who received him, to those who believed in his name, he gave the right to become children of God" (John chapter 1, verse 12). In the moment you welcome him, he welcomes you into his family. One day, he will welcome you into his heavenly home. So you see that Christianity puts forward a very simple invitation:

> In the moment you welcome him, he welcomes you into his family

You welcome him ... he welcomes you.

You refuse him ... he refuses you.

I wouldn't be writing this booklet if it was just to tell you how to get some immediate help. You may be helped wonderfully as God becomes your Father because you welcome his Son. But you will also have ultimate help for he will see you through the valley ... and beyond. He will be at the centre of a new and better world. And all his people will be there as well.

May he help you now and forever.